SPLINTER A. The First Wehrmacht issue.
Note the large brown splinters with small green drawings, and the white or
light grey background, with rain streaks on them.

SPLINTER A. On the left a quartershelter issued to all Wehrmacht units. On
the right a non regulation two piece suit of the same design.

AF322994

CAMOUFLAGED UNIFORMS OF THE WEHRMACHT 1930–1945

The first camouflage pattern was designed in Germany in 1929 for the regular quartershelter poncho (zeltbahn). The design consisted of splinter patterns, the larger ones in brown and the smaller ones in green. The background was grey with little green streaks representing rain. This pattern was very widely distributed throughout the Wehrmacht and used for triangular quartershelters (also buttoned up as ponchos), forage caps, field blouses in drill material, heavy padded parka, trousers, gloves, hoods, helmet covers and tents.

A second pattern appeared in 1941, often confused with Splinter Pattern A, but in which design smaller and more regular splinters were used, in effect a different design known as Splinter Pattern B. In 1942 a further design known as Splinter Pattern C was introduced, with the same design as Pattern A but with rougher edges to the splinter patterns and this was particularly used for padded materials. The Luftwaffe adopted the Splinter Pattern B for use by their paratroopers and ground fighters. The last Splinter Pattern was the Splinter D which is very rare because so few were ever distributed (see Selwyne Collection photo p. 28). This design featured a broken white background with khaki and brown patterns and fewer rain streaks. It appears that this design was originally intended to replace all the earlier patterns but that it was itself abandoned in favour of the famous, but little known "Leibermeister" design.

Another design, frequently seen on Luftwaffe troops, but also used by the Wehrmacht was the TAN WATER pattern. This design had a light brown background with many brown rain streaks. This design is the reverse of the Splinter A in that the larger patterns are in green and the smaller in brown. This design was not used for quartershelters or ponchos or forage caps but was often used for padded suits, gloves, hoods, snipers field blouses with mask etc. The final camouflage issued was a curious apron affair for Volksturm fighters in Berlin in 1945, made of long material with a hole for the head and tie on tapes.

The Wehrmacht camouflage panorama demonstrates the complexity of the problem for the Germany Army during World War Two and for other armies at a later date.

Initially camouflage was introduced for the triangular quartershelter known as the Zeltbahn. Three principal factories, two in Berlin, one in Stuttgart, prepared a special pattern for printing on the old Germany Army plain cotton cloth quartershelters. In 1938 this pattern was extended to helmet covers and the military manoeuvres of that year confirmed the efficiency of this splinter pattern camouflage. Although there were variations over the war years, with changes in the actual splinter pattern, hard and soft edges etc, right up to the end the Wehrmacht retained the basic splinter pattern, so different from the style adopted by the Waffen SS.

One can be certain that the basic design was efficient because even today, the Bulgarian and Polish armies wear a similar pattern (see Warsaw Pact Camouflage 1988). In 1960, the modern German Army, "Bundeswehr" of the German Federal Republic retained the Splinter A and Tan Water A for their first manoeuvres with the NATO Pact armies. One can be certain that it has nothing to do with nostalgia that these forces retained this camouflage. It was entirely due to the efficiency of the basic design.

TABLE OF CAMOUFLAGED ITEMS

SPLINTER A.

Regulation.

Quartershelter poncho—linen
Helmet Cover—light drill
Sniper Field Blouse
Parka trousers —padded material

Hood.
Gloves
Collection Tent —linen reinforced
Forage Cap.

Non-Regulation.

aprons – shirts – jacket – trousers.

SPLINTER B.

Parachute jump suit – drill material.
Luftwaffe ground jacket long – drill material.
Special helmet cover for paratroopers – helmet drill net.
Bandolier for cartridges.

SPLINTER C. = SPLINTER D.

Only known as padded material
and for sniper hooded field blouse (C).

TAN WATER A.

Never used for quartershelter poncho until Bundeswehr 1960. Never linen for material.

TAN WATER B.

Always drill material or padded.
Field Blouse, Helmet Cover, Parka, Trousers, Hood,
Gloves and a few rubber suits in Tan Water B for
anti-gas (apron, jacket with hood, trousers and rubber
shoes (coverall).

PARACHUTE MATERIAL.

COLLECTIVE TENTS SPECIAL PATTERN.

SPLINTER A. Poncho markings
Factories Anton Jöring, Warei Zeltbahn, Walter Reichert, DRP Berlin.

SPLINTER A. A heavily padded two piece suit of splinter design.

SPLINTER A. Light drill blouse in Splinter A with reversible white side.
DESCHOT Militaria Magazine Paris

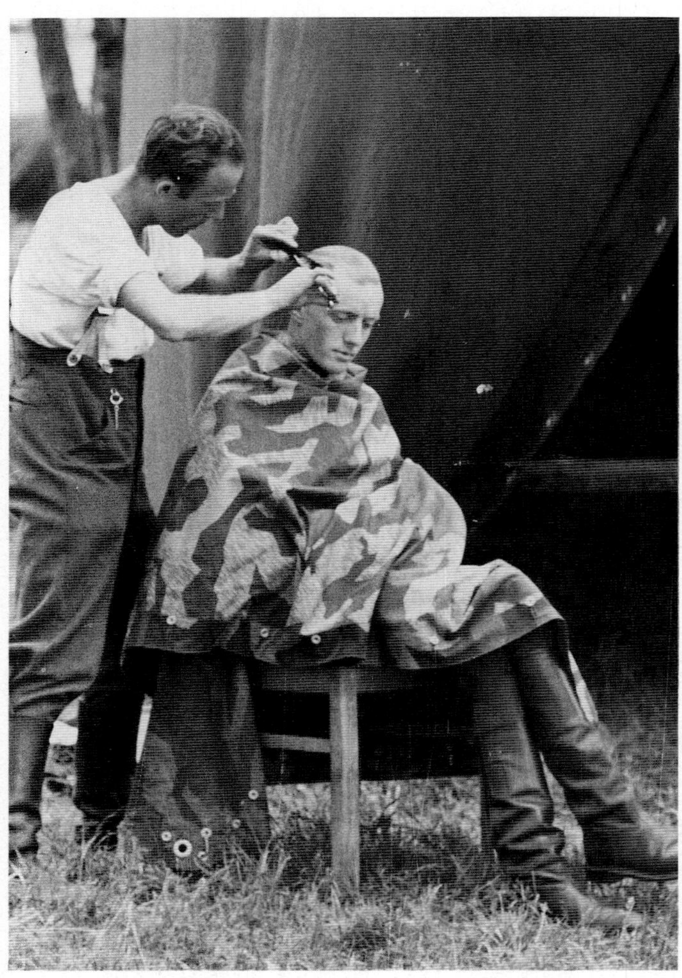 

SPLINTER A. Top Left: This German hairdresser uses the splinter zeltbahn as a cover for his customers. Top right and below: examples of the helmet cover using splinter A design in drill material with a reversible white side.

Photos: ECPA Paris

SPLINTER A. Above and below: Heavy padded reversible white parka in splinter design.

Photos: ECPA Paris

SPLINTER A. Non regulation two piece suit
made out of Zeltbahn material.

Balaclava hood and gloves worn
with a zeltbahn as a poncho.

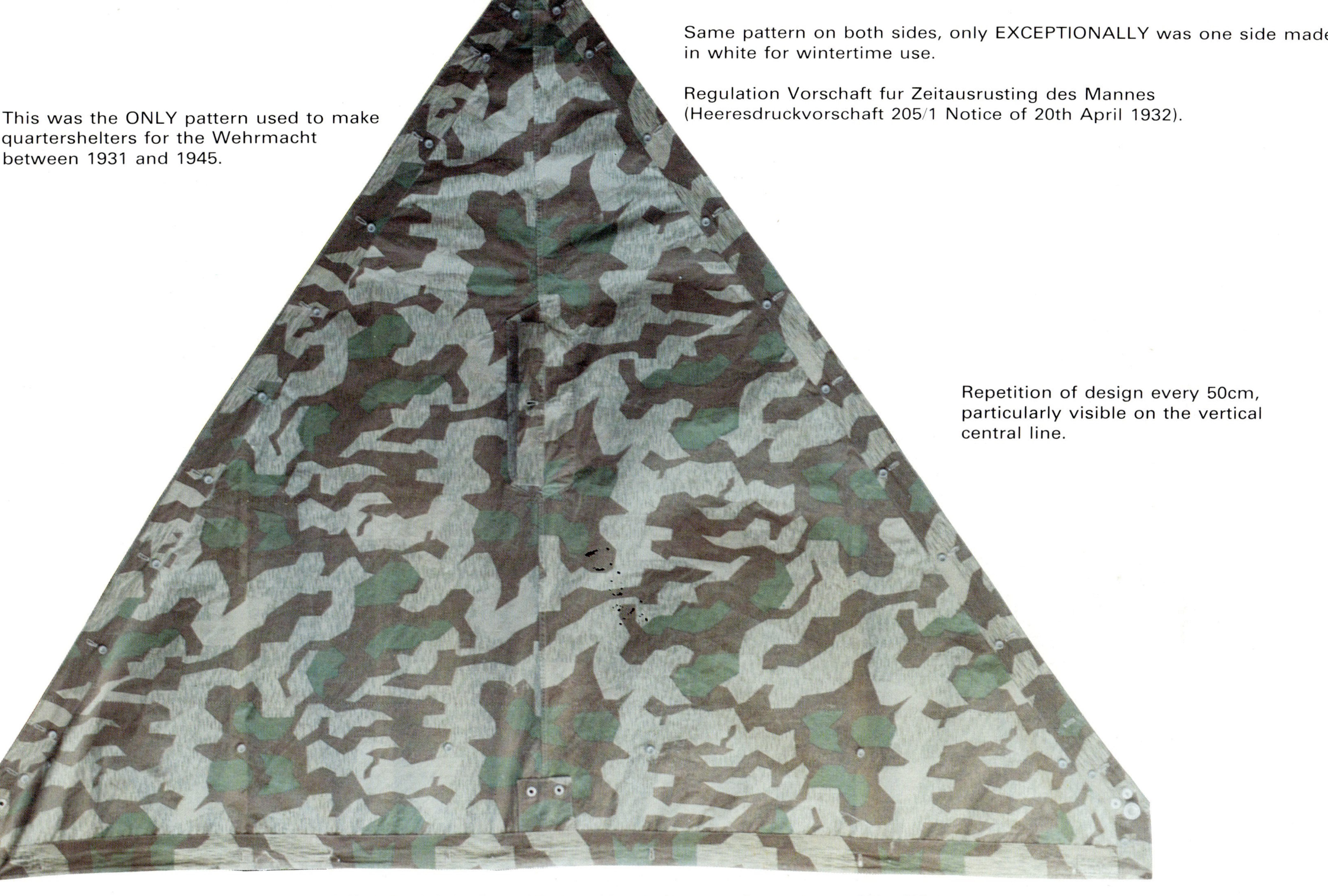

Same pattern on both sides, only EXCEPTIONALLY was one side made in white for wintertime use.

Regulation Vorschaft fur Zeitausrusting des Mannes (Heeresdruckvorschaft 205/1 Notice of 20th April 1932).

This was the ONLY pattern used to make quartershelters for the Wehrmacht between 1931 and 1945.

Repetition of design every 50cm, particularly visible on the vertical central line.

ZELTBAHN 1931. The ONLY quartershelter poncho pattern of the Wehrmacht which was always made of the splinter A design.
See study of Eric Lefevre, Militaria Magazine, Paris

SPLINTER A. Training exercises with zeltbahn on the back.

Photos: ECPA, Paris

SPLINTER A. Luftwaffe troops wearing the zeltbahn as a poncho.

SPLINTER B. Close up view of the design for paratroopers also showing the chin straps of the para helmet.

Photos: ECPA, Paris

SPLINTER B. Good view of this splinter design during inspection by General Student in Crete in July 1941.

SPLINTER B.
Paratrooper smock.

SPLINTER B. Ground fighter of Lutfwaffe
Field Division Hermann Göring.

GERMAN PARACHUTE RZ20. Markings read 10.210 2A 1 WERK 632 5172.

SPLINTER B PARATROOPERS.

SPLINTER B design in the centre. Splinter A on the right.

SPLINTER B. German paratroopers at rest in Tunis.

SPLINTER B. Motorcycle paratroopers in Tunis.

Photos: ECPA, Paris

SPLINTER B. Paratroopers on parade in Crete.

SPLINTER A. Wehrmacht.

SPLINTER B. WH PARATROOPERS.

SPLINTER C. WH Fluffy edged.

SPLINTER D. Rare Trial 1944.

TAN WATER A. Wehrmacht.

TAN WATER B.

SPLINTER C. This design was only used
for the Parka and Field Blouse.

SPLINTER C. Rear view of parka in this
splinter design.

On the left is a SPLINTER A design with a comparison showing the
SPLINTER C design on the right.   Photo: ECPA, Paris

SPLINTER C. The leading German escort is wearing a Field Blouse in Splinter
C design.

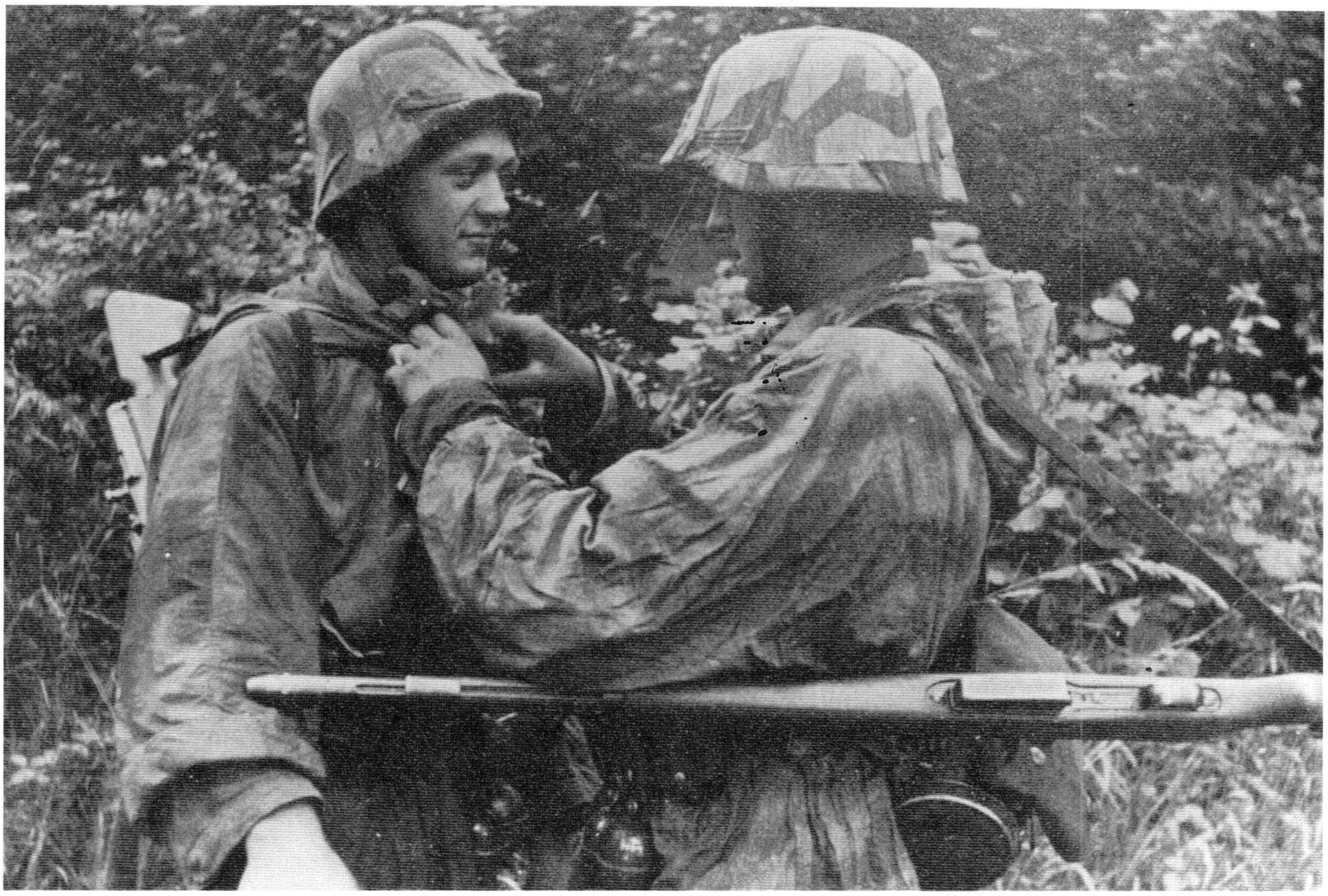

Above and below: Field Blouses made of Splinter C or Tan Water design.

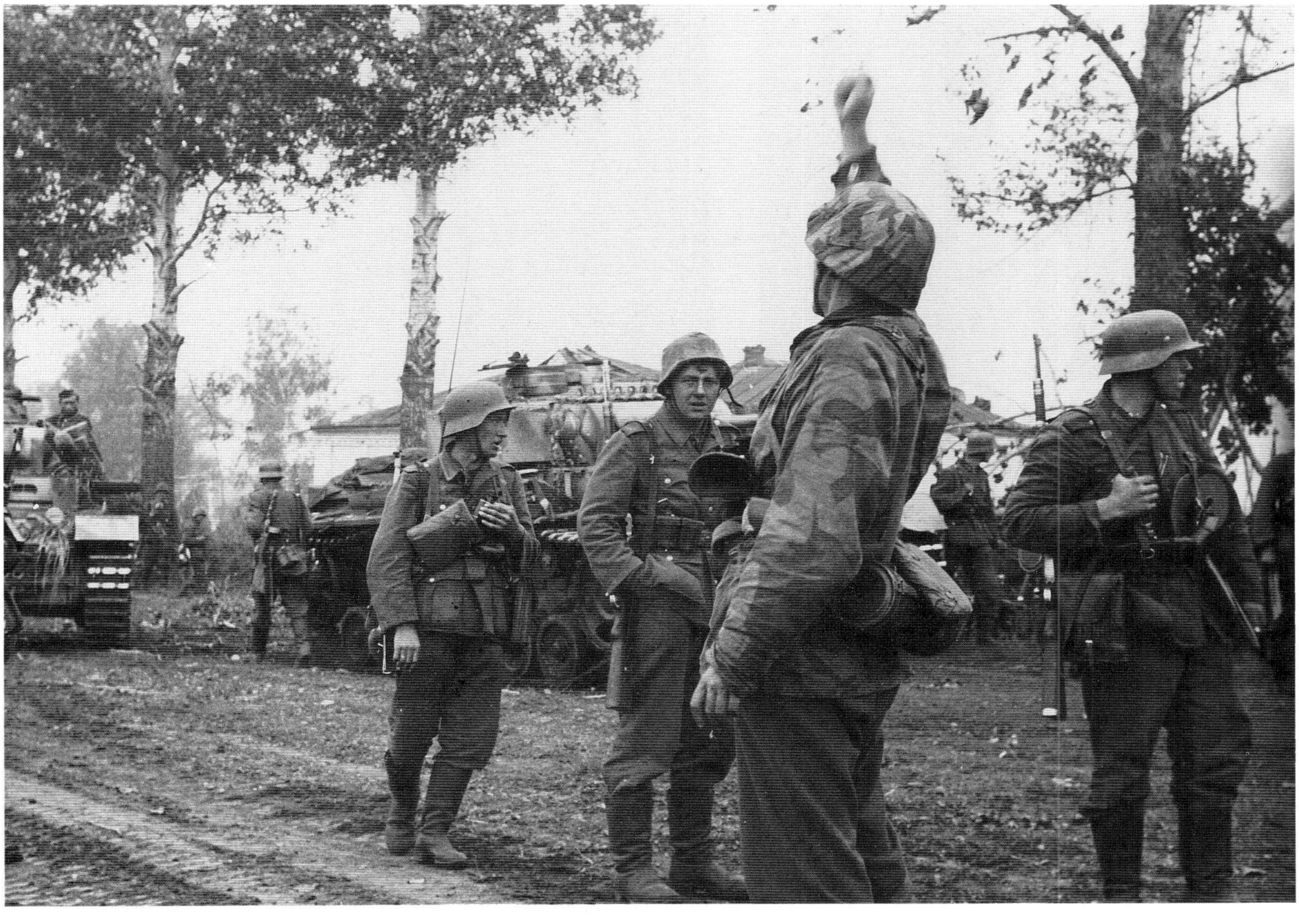

Photo ECPA, Paris

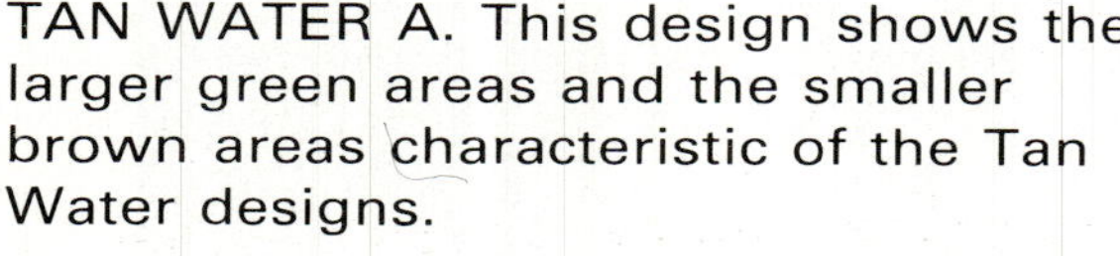

TAN WATER A. This design shows the larger green areas and the smaller brown areas characteristic of the Tan Water designs.

TAN WATER A. Winter padded suit. This design had soft burred edges.

TAN WATER A. A sample of a typical pink pattern of this design.

TAN WATER B with hard-edged splinter design. Paratroopers jump suit.
(Edmond Blanc Collection, Paris)

TENT CAMOUFLAGE. Above and below examples of this tent camouflage pattern.
Photo: ECPA, Paris

This parachute features a curious pattern unknown to the Wehrmacht.

SPLINTER A. This hospital collective tent is of splinter A pattern.

TAN WATER B. This illustration features the hard-edged tan water pattern.

This unknown pattern from Vervecken collection could perhaps be one of the trials patterns of 1945 or a cinema imitation?

SPLINTER B. For comparison the paratroopers and ground fighters smock.

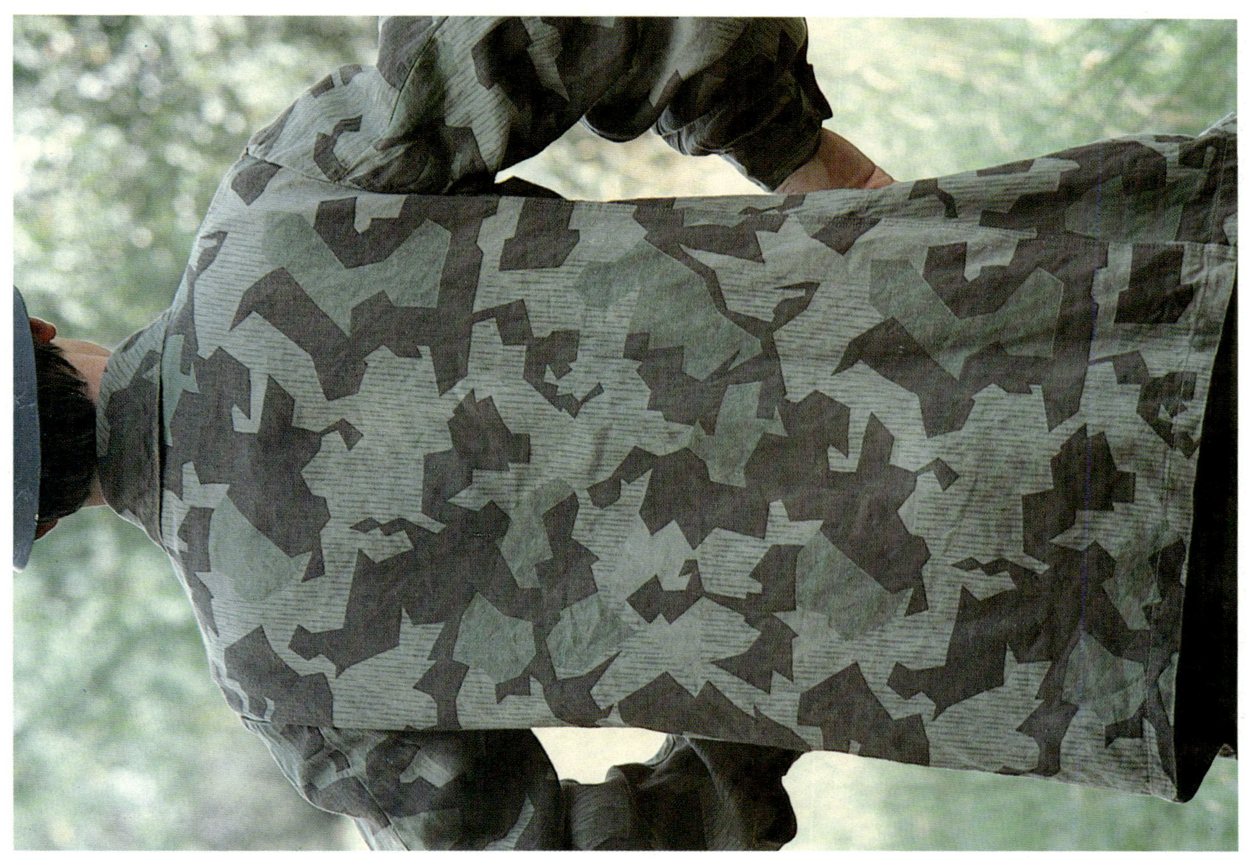

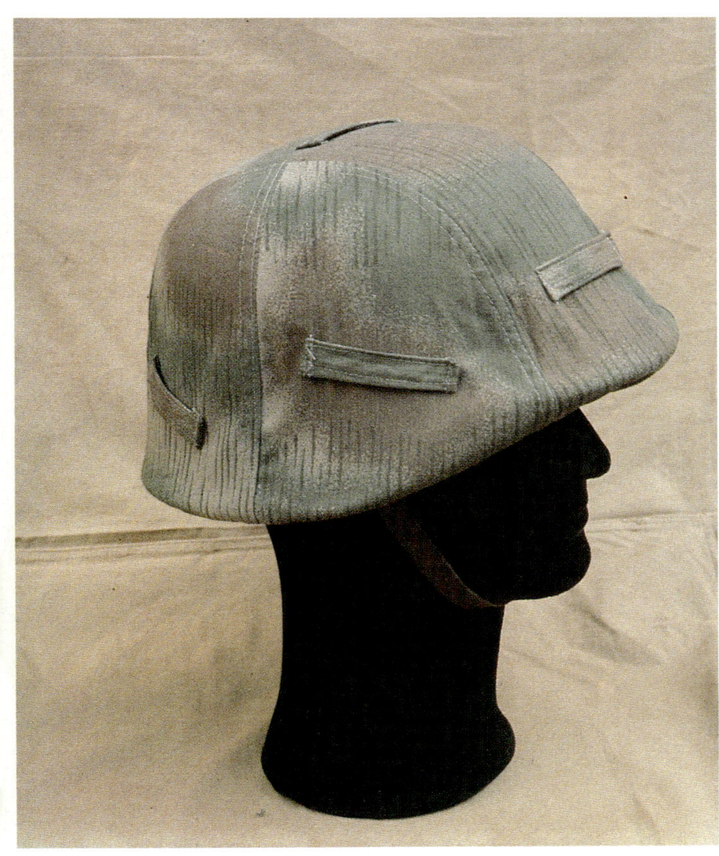

TAN WATER. Helmet cover.

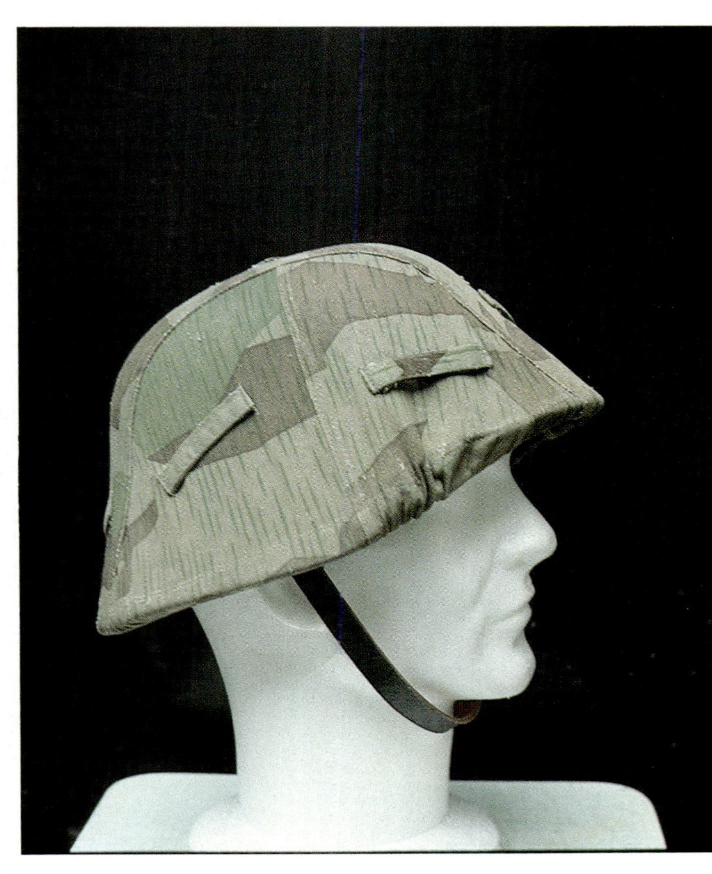

SPLINTER A. Helmet cover.

SPLINTER A. Above and below. Assembling the individual quartershelters made for more comfortable living accommodation.

VERY RARE 1937 photo
of camouflaged nets.

Below: Special
camouflaged nets of the
Wehrmacht in 1942.

Photo: ECPA, Paris

AMI photo collection
Smeets (Belgium) and
Chantrain (AMI
magazine).

VERY RARE 1945 pattern planned for all units, with reversible white side. An integration of all the old patterns since 1937.

Jack Selwyne Collection, London

Rear view of the rare 1945
Wehrmacht trial pattern parka.
Jack Selwyne Collection, London

The only picture of this
rare heavy suit was in
the film WHERE EAGLES
DARE where genuine
parkas in this design
were used.

SPLINTER A. Camouflage of a poncho sheltering a soldier telephonist.

Photos: ECPA, Paris

SPLINTER A. A Luftwaffe sergeant standing in front of an assembled poncho tent of splinter design.

SPLINTER A. Collective tents assembled from numerous individual ponchos.
Photos: ECPA, Paris

SPLINTER A. Panzer Grenadiers wearing field blouse and helmet covers of splinter design.

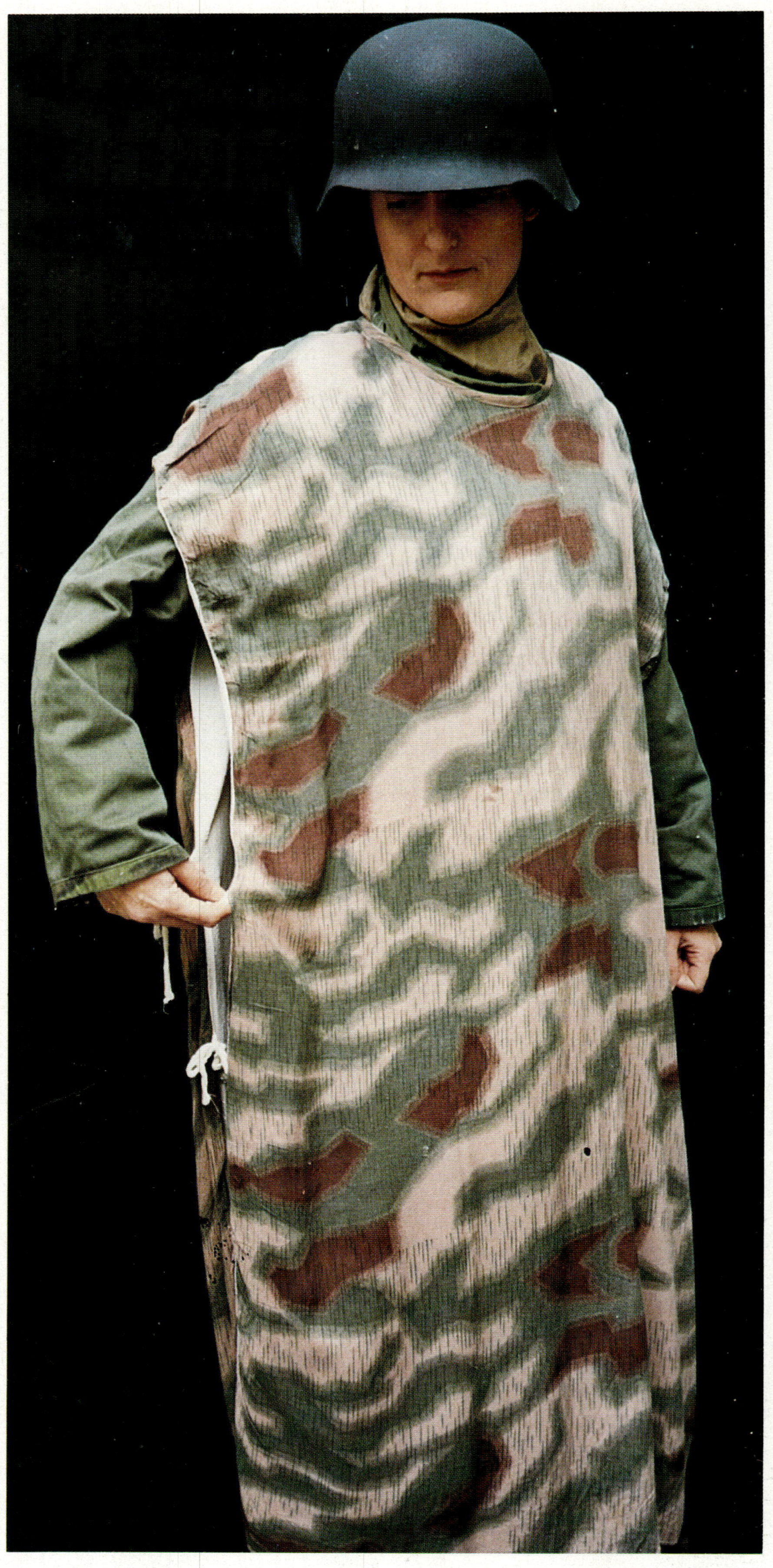

During the final days in Berlin, the administration issued to the Volksturm, this last and final camouflage pattern.

It was the end of a long, long camouflage story.